99 Things You Wish You Knew

Before®... Going To

Culinary School

Your guide to making the right choices
about your culinary education

Regina Varolli

www.99-series.com

The 99 Series
85 N. Main Street
Florida, NY 10921
646-233-4366

The author has done his/her best to present accurate and up-to-
date information in this book, but he/she cannot guarantee that the
information is correct or will suit your particular situation.

This book is sold with the understanding that the publisher and the
author are not engaged in rendering any legal, accounting or any
other professional services. If expert assistance is required, the
services of a competent professional should be sought.

First published by The 99 Series 2011

Ginger Marks Cover designed and Layout
DocUmeantDesigns www.DocUmeantDesigns.com

Cover Image Courtesy Jerome Landrieu, Barry Callebaut
Chocolate Academy

Dana Owens Copy Editor
http://www.dana-owens.com

Distributed by DocUmeant Publishing
For inquiries about volume orders, please contact:
99 Book Series, Inc.books@99-series.com

Library of Congress Cataloging-in-Publication Data
Varolli, Regina
        99 Things You Wish You Knew Before Going to
Culinary School: Cooking school, culinary school,
chef, culinary education.

LCCN - 2012936982

Printed in the United States Of America
ISBN-13: 978-1-937801-07-6   (paperback)
ISBN-10: 1937801071

WORDS OF PRAISE FOR...

---

99 Things You Wish You Knew Before®... Going To Culinary School

"Deciding to turn your passion into your career can be a daunting journey. Regina Varolli sheds some much needed light on many of the mysterious and elusive questions we all have faced. In <u>99 Things You Wish You Knew Before Going To Culinary School,</u> you are given all the tools you need to make an educated and honest decision about culinary school."—**Johnny Iuzzini, *Author <u>Dessert FourPlay</u>, James Beard award winner, head judge Top Chef Just Desserts***

"Finally, an answer to every question I've ever gotten about Cooking Schools. Before you write that tuition check be sure to make a smaller investment and read <u>99 Things You Wish You Knew Before Going To Culinary School</u>. It will help you make the right choices for you."
—Bobby Flay, *Chef/Owner Mesa Grill and Bar Americain*

*"All paths to **or around** culinary school should lead through Regina Varolli's definitive guide. The question of whether to go to culinary school is a scorchingly hot topic of debate in today's restaurant industry. And while Varolli doesn't take sides, she arms her readers to do so, ultimately making the right choice for them--and the industry."***—Will Blunt,** *Managing Editor, StarChefs.com*

"I want to give this book to every intern, budding writer and cook that asks me what to expect from culinary school. While all experiences are different, Regina Varolli has put together the best advice on this topic, gathered from top culinary professionals, and written it in a very clear and to-the-point manner that even the most naïve prospective professional cooks can

understand. From the realities of your first job out of school to learning the invaluable art of forming connections with other food professionals, this book will give you a great head start on your path to finding your dream job in the food world."—**Ben Mims, *Associate Food Editor, Saveur Magazine***

"A must read for any prospective student. Regina has carefully crafted a 'no nonsense' book that clearly outlines the reality of expectation, exposes the dangers of empty promises made by unscrupulous principals simply hell bent on gathering students and personal financial return no matter what. After reading these 99 Things that one needs to know, there is no excuse for lack of understanding, or exclaiming 'I didn't know.' It is all here, warts and all."—**Kerry Vincent, *"Food Network Challenge" Judge, Hall of Fame Sugar Artist, Oklahoma State Sugar Art Show Director, Author and freelance writer***

"This comprehensive book is a must-read for anyone even thinking about going to culinary school. Regina Varolli tells you everything you need to know about every aspect of the process,

with topics ranging from how to research schools to hidden costs to getting the most out of your culinary school experience while you're there. She even tells you what to expect after graduation. Read this book cover to cover before you send in that deposit!"—**Tish Boyle, cookbook author of The Cake Book**

"Before you even consider attending culinary school, you owe it to yourself (and your wallet) to read Regina's insights into joining one of the world's fastest growing professions."—**Matthew Stevens,** *Editor* **"Dessert Professional Magazine"**

"Spending a small amount on this book will ultimately save your bank account before making the financial commitment to culinary school. Read this book and I guarantee you will have a better understanding if the culinary industry is right for you."—**Jerome Landrieu,** *Director,* **Barry Callebaut Chocolate Academy**

"Successful chefs need great ingredients and the right tools to create culinary masterpieces. 99 Things You Wish You Knew Before Going To Culinary School is the first must-have tool!

Don't even think about culinary school until you've read this book."—**Francine Segan, I.C.E** *cooking instructor and James Beard nominated cookbook author*

"Regina Varolli offers honest, concise, and practical insight for anyone considering devoting their creative energy to culinary school. With her honest, no nonsense commentary it is clear that she has **walked the walk.**"—**Mike DeSimone and Jeff Jenssen,** *Entertaining and Lifestyle Editors, Wine Enthusiast Magazine, authors of The Fire Island Cookbook*

"This book perfectly provides the friendly but firm reality check that many kids need (and eventually will be most grateful for) before heading off to culinary school. Ms. Varolli speaks in useful home truths - not necessarily what an over-enthusiastic celebrity chef in-waiting will want to hear, but she comprehensively puts all sides and aspects of this potentially life-changing decision across in her own frank and very readable style.

Personally I would have loved someone to have warned me how boring some classes at one of the top culinary schools in London were going to be - I was totally unprepared for the dull days, and I wish I'd had Gina in my ear! Tell it how it is sister."—**Allegra McEvedy,** *Award-winning TV chef & best selling cookbook author*

DEDICATION

For Chris and Damien

CONTENTS

CHAPTER 3

CHAPTER 4

CHAPTER 5

ABOUT THE 99 SERIES

The 99 Series is a collection of quick, easy-to-understand guides that spell it all out for you in the simplest format: 99 points, one lesson per page. The book series is the one-stop shop for all readers tired of looking all over for self-help books. The 99 Series brings it all to you under one umbrella! The bullet point format that is the basis for all the 99 Series books was created purposely for today's fast-paced society. Not only does information have to be at our finger tips … we need it quickly and accurately without having to do much research to find it. But don't be fooled by the easy-to-read format. Each of the books in the series contains very thorough discussions from our roster of professional authors so that all the information you need to know is compiled into one book!

We hope that you will enjoy this book as well as the rest of the series. If you've enjoyed our books, tell your friends. And if you feel we need to improve something, please feel free to give us your feedback at www.99-series.com.

Helen Georgaklis
Founder & CEO, 99 Series

PREFACE

In 2008, thousands of students from the California Culinary Academy in San Francisco filed a class-action lawsuit against the school's parent corporation, Career Education, alleging that they were encouraged to borrow tens of thousands of dollars in student loans, and were led to believe they would swiftly move into high-paying jobs in the culinary industry, which would make it easy for them to repay their debt. When they graduated, they found that not only were they unable to find high-paying jobs, but the program itself had a bad reputation among hiring chefs. Many of the students claimed they couldn't even get a low-paying position.

The lawsuit, *Allison Amador et al. v. California Culinary Academy*, was born out of some serious investigative reporting by Eliza Strickland of *SF Weekly*. In her groundbreaking June 6, 2007 article entitled "Burnt Chefs" Strickland exposed the deceptive practices of the California Culinary Academy, having interviewed students, alumni, and former employees.

As was reported by Terence Chea of The Associated Press in his September 2011 article "Culinary School Grads Claim They Were Ripped Off," similar lawsuits have been filed against the California School of Culinary Arts in Pasadena and the Western Culinary Institute in Portland, Oregon—both of which are owned and operated by the same corporation as the California Culinary Academy. In each case, students claim they were urged to borrow tens of thousands of dollars while also being misled about the quality of the school, their job prospects, and their ability to repay their loans.

Sadly, these lawsuits point to a growing trend in culinary education as well as in the culinary industry. With so many people wanting to fulfill their passion for food by embarking on a career in the culinary industry, prospective students make easy marks and they graduate from culinary school with unrealistic expectations. Whether this is the fault of schools or the fault of a new breed of budding chefs that expect fame and fortune overnight—or a combination of both—it's a new reality that hasn't existed in previous generations.

With this book, I aim to arm today's generation of culinary hopefuls with the knowledge they'll need to never get fooled again, to never make life-changing mistakes because they didn't think through their decisions, and to know what they're really getting into when they choose to go to culinary school.

This book is neither intended to encourage nor discourage you from choosing to go to culinary school, nor is it intended to tell you which school you should attend. It *is* meant to help you make what will be one of the most important decisions of your career, and even your life. The choice to go to culinary school involves a lot of variables and I hope to help you navigate all of them so you can make wise, well-thought-out decisions about your culinary education.

ACKNOWLEDGMENTS

I would like to thank all of the chefs, pastry chefs, culinary students, line cooks, grunts, *commis*, kitchen assistants, food writers and editors whom I've spoken with over the years. Listening to your stories, the lessons you've learned, and your secrets for success have made this book something that will help a lot of people. Though you're not all quoted in these pages, you know who you are and I am forever in your debt.

For raising me in restaurants, I thank my mother. For showing me what the life of a chef can be, I must thank my father. For looking out for your baby sis and keeping us entertained at the restaurant, I thank my big sisters Becca and Nikki. The two of you have always been and will always be the most important people in my life.

Without my dear friend and other "sister" Ludy Green, her endless encouragement and willingness to connect me with her connections, my career—my life—would not be what it has become. Thank you Ludy!

I also thank Daria Siciliano. Only you know all of the ways we have relied on each other over the decades and I couldn't have written this book without your help.

Derek, Kyra, Chris, Karen and Damien ... No acknowledgment could possibly be complete without thanking all of you! In your own ways, each of you has propped me up, believed in me and kept me going whenever the going got tough—and that's more times than we can count.

Big thanks as well to my friend Thomas Schauer, food photographer extraordinaire, for taking time in his busy, globe-trotting schedule to do my head shot. And to Jerome Landrieu of the Barry Callebaut Chocolate Academy for the beautiful cover photo from his classroom.

I would also like to thank Lee Tachman, my business partner and friend, for introducing me to Helen Georgaklis and getting this ball rolling. If not for you, I literally wouldn't be writing this.

And of course, I thank Helen herself. Helen's support and wisdom, her friendship and faith in me, have meant so much on this life-changing journey called writing a book.

CHAPTER 1

WHY GO TO CULINARY SCHOOL

#1: The Purpose of Culinary School

Although culinary school may seem like a shortcut to a high-level position in the food industry, it's a mistake to assume this. The purpose of culinary school isn't to get ahead faster or to get a better job quicker than someone who didn't go to culinary school. You don't graduate from culinary school and instantly become a chef. Like any other field of study, after you graduate you still start out at the bottom.

Ultimately, you should choose to attend culinary school for your own personal reasons. It must fulfill a purpose for you and you alone. That being said, culinary school can serve several professional purposes. It can better prepare you to enter the job market, equip you to handle your professional responsibilities, and give you qualities, connections and experiences that will help you throughout your entire career.

#2: The Basics

Today's chefs strive for a level of creativity that goes way beyond previous generations of chefs. They often make it seem like there are no rules in cooking or baking. Icons like Chef Ferran and Pastry Chef Albert Adrià of the former elBulli and Grant Achatz of Alinea have pushed the boundaries of cooking to create plates that are artistic expressions. But like with any art form, you need to learn the basics before you can let your imagination run wild. Think about it this way: Picasso began by mastering how to draw a bowl of fruit and the human figure long before he developed his artistic style of Cubism.

Like Bobby Flay said to me, "You go to culinary school to learn the basics," and a good culinary school will teach them to you. Depending on the length of the program, it may or may not provide an in-depth study of any aspect of cooking or pastry, but that's not what you need when you're just getting started. What you need is to know how to scale and filet a fish, de-bone a chicken, make puff pastry, use a knife or piping bag, chop, julienne, and sauté. Learning the basics of cooking or pastry is indispensable. Without them, you'll trip up more often than you need to and that would make for one frustrating start to your career.

While you can learn the fundamentals by other means—practicing in your home kitchen or starting out at the very bottom in a professional kitchen—going to school does give you one decided advantage: you'll have an instructor to guide you and answer your questions; not a chef that will shout at or verbally abuse you when you do something wrong!

#3: Kitchen Experience

Unless you're lucky enough to have a fully-equipped home kitchen with tens, even hundreds of thousands of dollars of professional-grade equipment and tools, then stepping into your first job might be intimidating without a background in culinary school.

One important experience that culinary school offers is the simple opportunity to familiarize yourself with tools and equipment that you've likely never used and maybe even some that you've never seen. In culinary school, the classroom is a kitchen in which to learn, make mistakes, and become skilled at using every piece of equipment and every tool at your disposal.

Plus, it's a kitchen wherein you're working side-by-side with others; sharing a common space while maintaining your own space. You'll have to share ovens, burners, sheeters, mixers and counter space without messing up someone else's work or your own. The basic ability to function well with others in a kitchen is indispensable. Better to spill a pot of stock, drop a tray of macarons, or burn your hand in a classroom kitchen surrounded by sympathetic students than to make those same inevitable mistakes in a working kitchen where the people around you won't be so patient or understanding.

#4: Discipline

If there's one often-overlooked quality of a beginner in the culinary industry, it's discipline.

Chefs have to be disciplined and executive chefs demand discipline of everyone working under them. With sharp knives, hot ovens, and flaming burners, the last thing you (or anyone around you) needs is for you to run around the kitchen like a chicken with its head cut off. Your future kitchen boss also doesn't want you chatting up a storm, slacking off, or getting distracted.

The rigors of a professional kitchen demand discipline and school should provide it. When you're in school you'll face the pressure of working around others, standing for hours on end, and performing tasks well—no matter how dull—all without complaining or throwing in the towel.

Of course if you choose to forego school and jump right into the pressures of a professional kitchen, you'll learn discipline the hard way— and you'll likely get shouted at by everyone above you. Thing is, even coming out of school, you'll probably get the same treatment going into your first position. That's just the nature of the beast.

#5: Cleanliness

Whoever said that cleanliness is close to godliness must have worked in a professional kitchen.

In a professional kitchen, you simply cannot be a slob. Not only is it unsanitary, but making a mess is inefficient and cleaning it up is time-consuming—all three of which are major issues in a professional kitchen. In culinary school, you're expected to clean as you go rather than wait until you're finished to clean up all of your tools, bowls and pans. The cleanliness of your counter space, floor, and even your chef's whites, *while you're working*, are all a reflection of your professionalism and organizational abilities.

Some schools actually include cleanliness in their grading system. Even if they don't, you'll still somehow be judged on how spotless you keep your work station. I've know people who were complete slobs in their home kitchens despite being talented cooks, then when they came out of culinary school, they worked cleaner than they (or I) ever thought possible.

#6: Camaraderie

Like boot camp before heading off to battle, in culinary school you're thrown in with a bunch of people you don't know who are all learning the same things you are, facing the same challenges, and hoping for the best futures. In a literal and figurative sense, in school you're just not alone.

Even with the healthy competition you'll get in any culinary program, there's a huge feeling of camaraderie among students. You're surrounded by people who have all chosen the same path, the same career, and the same school. On the hardest of days, you'll always have someone who can relate to you.

This sense of camaraderie exists in most professional kitchens where the work is long and hard; where it's passion, not a fat paycheck, that keeps you coming back for more. The thing that makes camaraderie different in culinary school is that everyone is starting off in the same place at the same time and nobody is above or below you.

#7: Connections

Jody Eddy, former Executive Editor of *Art Culinaire* magazine and a culinary school grad, told me that the connections she made in culinary school became an important career resource after school. It's the same no matter what you study; your fellow students today become your professional network tomorrow.

Like in any professional field, your success can often depend on your connections. Connections contact you when they hear about job opportunities that might interest you, they reach out to you to join their team for a competition, they talk about you and your work to people within the industry. While you'll make and ideally nurture connections throughout your entire career, there's something unique about the connections you make based on the camaraderie of being fellow students.

When you go to culinary school and you're thrown into the same circumstance with a bunch of like-minded individuals, you'll never forget each other. And connections that never forget you and the experiences you shared just starting out can be the most valuable connections of all.

#8: Exposure

Going to a good culinary school gives you the chance to be exposed to so many diverse aspects of the culinary industry as well as the diversity inherent in being a chef today. Depending on the school's curriculum and extracurricular activities, you'll be exposed to many things you normally wouldn't experience when you start out at the bottom in a kitchen.

Take a pastry program as an example. When you're exposed to the fundamentals of bread baking, cake baking and decorating, Viennoiserie, chocolate, and more, you get the chance to discover which of these specialties you like most and are best at doing. Then you can come out of school and look for a position that will allow you to focus on the particular field in pastry in which you want to build your career.

Culinary school can also give you the opportunity to participate in competitions, attend industry events and seminars, and to experience an internship or apprenticeship. Many culinary schools even have their own restaurants, bakeries, student clubs, and events. Take these opportunities while you can! The more you expose yourself to everything that's available to you as a student, the better your skills will be and the more deeply and diversely involved you'll become with all the ways you can build your career beyond just studying and working in a kitchen.

#9: Confidence

So many chefs have told me that walking into a professional kitchen on their first day of work was more than a little intimidating. You're told what to do without explanation and expected to do it without assistance. What can save you as you enter the culinary workforce is your level of confidence.

Going to school, learning the fundamentals of your craft, familiarizing yourself with the trappings of a professional kitchen, and already knowing how to work cleanly gives you a level of confidence in yourself that you likely won't have without school.

But beware of the line between confidence and cockiness. Just because you're a graduate of a culinary program doesn't make you a chef on day one, nor does it mean you know everything there is to know about your craft. As *Ace of*

Cakes Duff Goldman put it to me, "You need to really believe in yourself beyond the normal self-confidence. But at the same time, if you're not the executive chef, you better button that shit up because they just don't want to hear it!"

CHAPTER 2

THE COST OF CULINARY SCHOOL

#10: A Significant Investment

Let's be honest. Culinary school today can set you back a small fortune, especially the vastly popular six-month, intensive programs. Culinary school can cost upwards of $50,000, and that's no small investment considering it can take years to make financial gains in the industry.

For many, the investment is well worth it. In today's market, you could have trouble even getting your foot in the door without a certificate, diploma or degree, at least not in the door of a paying, entry-level cooking or pastry position. But financing your education may not be worth it to you if you're fine starting out at the very bottom as a dishwasher, or even working for free to prove yourself.

Cesar Ramirez, Chef/Owner of the Michelin three-star Chef's Table at Brooklyn Fare never went to school. Instead, he got his start by walking into a kitchen and convincing the chef to give him a shot working for free for three days. He worked his butt off, didn't complain, and kept his focus. After three days slaving away for no pay, the chef hired him into the lowest position in the kitchen.

#11: Beware the Real Cost

The cost of culinary school goes beyond just the check you'll write (or the money you'll borrow) to pay for tuition. It includes your cost of living when you're in school.

If you're in a full-time culinary program and you don't have the time to even work a part-time job, then the real cost of culinary school includes your cost of living. Unless you're still living with your parents, you'll have rent and bills to pay and groceries to buy. In any case, you'll have transportation costs, clothes to buy, and the money you'll spend on entertainment.

Tish Boyle, author, food stylist and editor of *Dessert Professional* magazine, told me this about the real cost of her culinary education— which she did at La Varenne Ecole de Cuisine in Paris: "Going to culinary school in Paris was a flaming fortune. By the time I arrived, the exchange rate had become less favorable and my tuition had gone up quite a bit, to around $21,000 for 9 months (and this was in the 1980s). And that didn't include living expenses, which were also very high."

#12: Hidden Costs

While all culinary schools should make the financials clear to potential students, they don't. So know this: tuition might not cover everything you'll need to pay in order to enroll in a program.

In culinary school, you have to wear a uniform and this can be an additional expense. Sometimes costly "lab fees" are tacked on to the tuition and of course there are text books to buy. And more often than not, you'll either need or want to buy a set of your own kitchen tools or knives and something secure in which to carry them.

Take the time to uncover all the hidden costs beyond tuition at any school you're considering. Find out exactly which tools you'll need to buy and which tools they'll have available to share. Also consider that you might want to supply your own so you don't have to share. Add up all of these expenses and you'll have a clear picture of how much enrolling in a program is going to set you back, beyond just tuition.

#13: Meals & Housing

Today a lot of culinary programs are offering affordable housing and meal plans to their students. If you think you want to relocate to study culinary or pastry arts, it will definitely be worth your time to look into programs that offer student housing and meals.

Even if you're not relocating for school, it's not a bad idea to check out this option anyway. For all you know, the rent on your current apartment might be higher than the housing at your future school and meal plans may turn out to be a cheaper option than feeding yourself. While Tish Boyle paid "a flaming fortune" to study in Paris at La Varenne, she also made this point: "At least I knew I was going to have one good meal—usually with wine—every day at school."

#14: Community Colleges

Wherever you live, chances are there's a community college near you that offers a degree, diploma or certificate program in culinary or pastry arts. Mindful of the ever-growing popularity of culinary studies, many community colleges have ramped up their culinary programs and now offer highly competitive degrees without hugely expensive tuition.

In all fifty states, community college systems were created to provide affordable, accessible education for everyone and they haven't changed that mission when it comes to culinary and pastry arts programs. So going to a community college to study cooking or pastry is far more affordable than attending a private institution. While the cooking or baking programs at community colleges most often cost more than studying, say, English Literature, they're still far less expensive than private school alternatives. If you're thinking of moving to a different state to pursue your studies, you'll want to check if the community college you're interested in has a higher tuition for non-residents.

Just don't think you have to sacrifice the quality of your education. There are plenty of community college programs that are equal to and even better than expensive, private culinary schools!

#15: Career & Technical Programs

Even more affordable than community colleges are career and technical education programs. While some states lump their career-tech into the community college system, other states offer vocational training that's even more affordable than community college. For example, in California alone there are nearly one-hundred Regional Occupational Centers and Programs that provide career and technical education.

One national program, the Job Corps, offers free training in the culinary and baking arts. You have to be between the ages of 16-24 to enroll in a Job Corps program, but if you're in that age group and the high cost of culinary training is discouraging you, it's worthwhile to see if there's a Job Corps Training Center near you (or even relocate to be near one).

Max Brenner, "the bald chocolate guy" who created a chocolate empire with shops in the U.S., Singapore, Philippines, and Israel, got his culinary training in a government-subsidized, vocational-technical program. From what's often considered a humble beginning, Brenner was nevertheless able to build a career that places him among the most financially successful people in the culinary industry today.

If you're still in high school and you already have a passion for the kitchen, you can enroll in a vocational-technical training program in your junior and senior years. More often than not, these programs won't cost you any tuition and they'll give you a huge head start when you graduate from high school. Plus, you can check out an organization called C-CAP (Careers through Culinary Arts Program). C-CAP aims to serve kids in challenging circumstances, and they operate high school programs across America. For twenty years, C-CAP has worked with high school students, connecting them with chefs, vocational training, and even internships.

#16: Private Not-for-Profit

While not as inexpensive as community college programs, private not-for-profit institutions will set you back less cash than their for-profit competition. Not-for-profit educational institutions are categorized and taxed differently by both federal and state government because their stated mission is not to make a profit, but to provide an education. Often times at a private not-for-profit school, a greater emphasis is placed on the curriculum rather than the financial bottom line.

You can find out if a private institution is not-for-profit simply by asking someone in the admissions office. Don't be shy about asking this question. Rushing into a program without knowing what its mission could be—education or profit—isn't the smartest move you can make!

#17: Private For-Profit

The most expensive culinary and pastry programs around are the for-profit institutions. Whether it's a six–month, full-time program that comes with a $40,000 tuition or a two-year program costing roughly the same or more over a longer period of time, you'll want to think hard before you enroll. After all, these were the kinds of schools that I talked about in my introduction ... the ones that got sued.

Unless you're one of the fortunate few who have wads cash just sitting around and you won't miss it if you spend it, then you're probably going to have to take out hefty student loans to pay for your private, for-profit education. While it may seem painless to borrow that kind of money, it does come with interest, and you will eventually have to pay it all back.

Paying more doesn't necessarily mean getting more. One of the biggest criticisms of private, for-profit culinary schools today is that they're so concerned with making a profit that they churn out graduates regardless of how much they've actually learned. In some cases, they won't hold students back or make them repeat any section of the training, even if they obviously didn't learn the material. In other words, if you pay, you pass.

Not all private, for-profit schools crank out graduates, some actually have grading systems. The Notter School of Pastry Arts in Orlando, FL gives students grades on a scale of A to F, and students must repeat, and pass, sections they failed before they can earn a diploma. So it's worth asking potential schools if they do the same.

#18: Getting What You Pay For

The bottom line is, whatever type of culinary program you choose, you want to be damn sure you're getting what you pay for. Really take the time to look into the schools you're interested in attending. Find out exactly what they offer in their curriculum, how many hours you'll spend in the kitchen versus the classroom, and how many hours are devoted to each segment of the curriculum.

Most community college websites have their course catalogues available online so you can easily see what classes you'll be taking. Private institutions often provide a detailed break-down of the program hours and the areas of study as well. If you can't find this information on a program's website, then call the school and ask them to send you the information or tell you over the phone.

Whatever you do, don't enroll in any program, send off a check, or borrow money unless you know *exactly* what you'll be studying. It's one thing to have buyer's remorse over a pair of shoes, but quite another to have it over an education!

CHAPTER 3

TYPES OF CULINARY PROGRAMS

#19: Culinary Arts

The most common culinary program in America is culinary arts. Whether it's actually referred to as Culinary Arts, Culinary Studies, Culinary Technology, or Foodservice will depend on the institution, but with the popularity of careers in the kitchen, there's no shortage of programs to choose from.

Culinary arts trains students in savory cooking and may or may not touch on dessert and pastry. So it's important to know whether you want to be a savory or pastry chef before you enroll in a program. In a savory kitchen, you'll be butchering, shucking, and deboning, cutting the heads off lobsters, gutting pigs, and doing a whole bunch of other potentially off-putting stuff. Some people just don't want to do this kind of work. In an interview with Johnny Iuzzini, *Top Chef Just Desserts* judge and author, he said he chose pastry over savory school because he just didn't want to do all that butchering.

If you're really unsure about whether to study savory or pastry, spend time doing the grunt work in a savory kitchen and then do the same in a pastry kitchen. If you don't ask to get paid, it shouldn't be hard to find somewhere that will let you do this. It'll be the best thing you could do to help you make up your mind between pastry and savory.

#20: Pastry Arts

While the growing popularity of pastry, dessert, and cake has led to a jump in the number of pastry programs around the county, there are still less pastry arts programs than culinary arts programs. So you may have to look a bit harder to find the pastry program that's right for you.

Pastry and baking programs can teach very different skills depending on where you choose to study. Some programs emphasize French pastry where you'll learn things like Viennoiserie, French macarons and cannelé. Others emphasize American pastry and baking and spend a lot of time on things like special occasion cakes, decorating with fondant and gum paste, and making cookies and muffins. Still other programs try to give you a broad education and will touch on as much as they possibly can.

With a pastry and baking program, it's really important to know the exact curriculum. While the basics of savory cooking are pretty much the same no matter what kind of chef you want to become, the fundamentals of pastry and baking can be very different depending on where you want to take your career. Consider that bread baking is an art and craft in and of itself, as is cake decorating, making chocolate bonbons, baking croissants and breakfast pastries, and on and on. So think about your long-term career plans in the diverse world of pastry and then choose a program that gives you the kind of fundamental training that will best help get you on that particular path.

#21: Culinary Management

Especially in the community college setting, you'll see a lot of schools that offer either Culinary Arts, Culinary Management, or both (or it might be called Foodservice Management or Hospitality Management). While both of these types of programs will teach the fundamentals of cooking, there's a big difference you'll want to consider before choosing between the two.

In a culinary management program, you're going to take more classes that focus on business management than you would if you just studied culinary arts. In a straight culinary arts program, you probably won't get any management classes at all, but you may not want any. Culinary management classes can be helpful in the long run because they'll teach you about important things like inventory and ordering, cost control and pricing, staffing and scheduling, and other aspects of running a kitchen operation beyond the stove.

While you won't need to know how to be the manager in your first job after school (or even your first ten jobs), knowing the business side of a kitchen can make you a better employee because you'll understand your role in the overall operation. Plus, as anyone who wants to be a chef hopes to become an executive chef, a degree or diploma in Culinary Management can give you a more knowledgeable starting point.

#22: Six-Month to One-Year Programs

On average, the shortest program you'll find that will award a certificate or diploma is going to take up six months of your life. Generally speaking, six-month programs are full time, Monday through Friday, and at least six hours each day. Quite often these programs refer to themselves as "intensive" because they try to cover as much as they can within such a short time frame. In a six-month program, you'll likely get a limited amount of training in a lot of different areas, moving quickly from one part of the curriculum to another and then another.

A large percentage of private, for-profit institutions offer six-month, intensive training programs, and while they'll get you in and out quickly, you may not want to feel as if you're rushing to learn as much as possible in as little time as possible. You may want to have the opportunity to spend a bit more time delving deeper and getting more practice.

In a nine-month to one-year program, you'll cover more ground than you will in six months and you'll also get in more practice time on each aspect of the curriculum. If you want to earn a degree rather than a certificate or diploma, some programs offer intensive, one-year training at the end of which you'll earn an associate's degree. However, there isn't a single six-month program that offers an associate's.

#23: Two-year Degree Programs

If earning your associate's degree matters to you, then your best—and sometimes only—option will be attending a two-year program. The good news is that between community and technical colleges and private institutions like The Art Institutes, there's no shortage of two-year, degree-offering programs from which to choose.

There are some obvious benefits to two-year degree programs. For one, at the end of your studies you'll have an academic degree and this can be very useful if you want to take your culinary training beyond a career in a kitchen. Another benefit is that while you'll be in school for a longer period of time, you won't be in class as many day-to-day hours as you would be in a six-month program, so it'll be easier to hold a job while you're in school. A two-year degree program will also require you to take classes beyond just cooking or culinary management. To earn your degree, you'll have to take some general education classes and these will broaden your horizons and expand your intellect.

One cool thing about doing a two-year program at a community college is that you can choose to take elective classes that might not relate directly to culinary or pastry arts, but can still help you develop skills that will make you a better chef. For example, pastry chefs might like to take a drawing class or a class on color theory, as both of these will improve artistic ability—something paramount to pastry. When you attend a two-year community college, you can explore all the classes they offer outside of your major and take a few that will strengthen the kinds of skills you'll need for a successful culinary career.

#24: Four-Year Degree Programs

If you want to earn a bachelor's degree, a four-year program is your only choice. In today's wildly popular culinary industry though, so many young people cheat themselves out of the opportunity for higher education in their rush to be the next great chef. While the culinary industry isn't one that requires a bachelor's degree to make it big, if you're someone who still wants a traditional liberal arts education, then give some serious thought to earning your bachelor's.

One of the most respected culinary schools in the country is The Culinary Institute of America (CIA), a four-year, degree-granting institution. Executive chefs have told me over and over again that CIA graduates are among the best-educated and well-prepared new hires they have. This is largely because in a four-year program nothing is rushed, nothing is brushed over—or brushed aside—and you have years to study both the depth and breadth of culinary or pastry arts.

While there aren't a lot of four-year culinary schools compared to the two-year programs, they can be well worth seeking out, relocating, and giving four years of your life to them because they have the potential to give you back so much more than you could possibly get from any shorter program.

The choice to earn a bachelor's degree is yours alone. You don't need it, but if you want it for your own reasons, you'll end up with a better grasp of the fundamentals, better preparedness, and more confidence in your skills than you can get from just about any other program.

#25: Internship & Apprenticeship Programs

No matter where you choose to study and no matter how much time you want to devote to your education, I can't over-emphasize the importance of doing an internship or apprentice-ship. I'd almost go so far as to say that before you get your first real job, you *must* do one, but in this business there are no set rules—so I won't say that!

Not all culinary programs include these while some programs rely heavily on them. You can even find some that base half of your training on your internship or apprenticeship. The American Culinary Federation offers an apprenticeship program and some culinary programs include an apprenticeship that runs concurrently throughout your time in school. Both are worth looking into to soak up some real-world experience along with—or instead of—formal education.

Damien Herrgott, a third-generation pastry chef, never went to culinary school yet he spent years working for Pierre Hermé in Paris and is now the Executive Pastry Chef and partner at the acclaimed Bosie Tea Parlor in New York City, as well as a *Dessert Professional* 2012 Top Ten Pastry Chef in America. But, like most French chefs and pastry chefs, he did a two-year apprenticeship, and today he welcomes interns into his own kitchen. Herrgott told me, "There are experiences you'll get by interning or apprenticing in a kitchen that you just won't get in school. It isn't by learning theory and practicing something only a few times that makes someone comfortable in their work. You have to do things hundreds of times, over and over again, and you'll only get that experience working in a kitchen."

#26: Special-Focus Programs

Today's culinary landscape is so diverse that depending on what you want to do with your career, you may want to seek out a program that can offer you some kind of special focus or emphasize a particular aspect of your broader training.

For example, one specialization that's huge in today's market is cakes and cake decorating. This sector of the industry has exploded thanks in large part to shows like *Food Network Challenge*, *Ace of Cakes*, and *Cake Boss*. As a result, there are quite a few pastry and baking programs that emphasize this area of training. But whatever area you want to spend more time studying, make sure the school you choose offers that kind of special focus.

On the savory side, many community colleges offer training that leads to special certifications in catering, private chef, or banquet chef. And there are entire institutions devoted to specializations, like The Raw Food Chef in Fort Bragg, California, Bauman College of Holistic Nutrition & Culinary Arts in Santa Cruz, California, and The Natural Gourmet Institute for Health & Culinary Arts in New York City.

The point here is that whatever you might want to specialize in, it's worth your time researching programs that can boost your skills in everything from chocolate, sugar, or decorating, to sushi, pizza or pasta, and even vegan and vegetarian cuisine.

#27: Combining Studies

Sometimes a person's interests go beyond just cooking or baking and they have a passion for more than one discipline. Sometimes these disciplines compliment each other, like with art studies and pastry arts or culinary arts and wine studies. Sometimes they don't, but you still have a passion for more than just culinary or pastry arts and a desire to broaden your educational horizon.

If that's the case with you, then pursuing an education at a community college or university will be your best bet. At a community college or university, you can double major or major in one discipline and minor in another. Depending on your long-term career plans, it can be very handy to study both culinary arts and hospitality management or wine studies, or culinary arts and journalism or marketing. But you just won't get this opportunity in a six-month or one-year program that only teaches you fundamental cooking or baking skills.

Besides wanting to pursue more than one passion, pursuing a double major or a major/minor program in two related (or even unrelated) fields will definitely broaden your career choices and provide you with a fall-back career in the event that one day you decide to step away from the kitchen.

CHAPTER 4

RESEARCHING SCHOOLS

#28: Getting Started

There are so many culinary schools and programs in America today that the thought of doing some serious research into them can be overwhelming. But you can't let the wide range of choices stop you from doing thorough research. Instead, it should motivate you!

Before you start researching, take the time to think about all of the things I discuss in this book. Make a list if you like and note of all the variables as they apply to you as an individual. This way you can narrow the list of programs you'd be interested in even before you begin your research.

Having a clear idea of what you want, how you want it, where you want it, and even what you can afford will definitely cut down on the amount of time you'll spend doing research and it'll help you to make the best decision for you.

#29: School Websites

If you want to learn about a particular program, go to the school's website. Most schools have taken the time to create informative websites that tell you everything about the curriculum, cost, instructors, extra-curricular activities, and they'll even tell you if the school has a student-run restaurant or bakery (or even hotel!). School websites should also provide contact information so you can pick up the phone and talk to some-one or fire off an email with your questions.

Take the time to examine the course catalog or the details of the curriculum so you'll know if what they're teaching is actually what you want to learn. Some community colleges offer what they call "Culinary Arts," but the curriculum turns out to be thin on actual kitchen time and instead you spend a lot of time learning theory in a classroom.

Another telling thing about a school's website in relation to its culinary program is exactly how much effort they've put into developing an informative online presence. If you go to a school's website and they don't even have a page devoted to the culinary program, the lack of information on the website might say a lot about the potential lack of quality in the program. Conversely, don't let a flashy website make you conclude it's the best school around. You're still going to need to dig deeper!

#30: Program Brochures

Especially among the well-funded and often expensive private schools, glossy brochures have been developed to both inform and to lure potential students. But many community college and university programs have developed brochures as well, so don't assume they don't have one. The culinary school industry seems as competitive as the culinary industry itself and the program brochure helps schools to compete for your business.

Always check to see if the school you're interested in has a PDF brochure to download. If you don't see a PDF brochure, then send an email or call the school to see if they have one to send you. Some schools have whole information packets in addition to their brochures, and trust me, they'll be happy to send them to you by snail mail.

Don't overlook the brochure or the information packet, they're invaluable sources of detailed information about any program. But also know that these kinds of materials are meant to sell a school, to get you to want to choose them over other schools. In a way, they're like advertising and there isn't always truth in advertising. They'll all present their schools as the best place to go, so be prepared to read beyond the hype, focus on the facts, and always keep your own personal needs and wants foremost in your mind.

#31: Making Calls

At some point in your research, you will have to pick up the phone and make some calls. You'll want to call the schools you're thinking about attending so you can speak with people in both the admissions office and the program office.

You can't avoid it and you can't just text message these people. In an age where the telephone seem to be a dying form of communication, when it comes to choosing the right school for you, there's no substitute for the good old phone call.

If you just hate making calls, do yourself the favor of thinking about what you want to know from whomever it is you're calling before you call them. Write down your questions and concerns before you pick up the phone. You'll have some questions you want to ask every school and some specific questions you'll want to ask a given individual school, so you may have to approach each call with its own prep work.

It's not just schools that you can call; you can also call some restaurants, hotels, bakeries, and other foodservice businesses located near the schools you're considering. Why? Because you can ask them what they think or have heard about the particular schools you're considering. Among industry professionals, different schools have different reputations, but the schools themselves won't necessarily tell you what the chefs who hire their graduates really think about the quality of their program.

#32: Visiting Campuses

No matter how wonderful a school's website, brochure or information package is, no matter who you've spoken with over the phone, nothing takes the place of seeing the physical campus, the kitchen facilities, and the people, up close and personal.

Whether you decide to take part in a formal information session organized by the school or just pop on over to the campus and poke around on your own—or do both—this is an important step you shouldn't skip. If you don't live in an area that has a lot of schools to visit within a relatively short distance, then you'll have to narrow down your list to serious contenders before you venture onto campuses.

For those of you considering schools that are so far away you'd need to fly or drive two days to get there, make sure you've really done all your research first and are certain it's a school that's truly worth your time and money just to visit. But do whatever you must to make the visit despite the distance. In some ways, it's even more important to visit a far away place before you attend because not only will you want to see the campus on which you'll be studying, you'll want to see the city or town in which you'll be *living*! For some people, that can be as much of a deciding factor as the quality of the campus. Can you imagine enrolling in a school, sending off your check or borrowing a chunk of money, and then relocating to a new place only to discover you hate it?

#33: Talking to Students

Some of the best feedback and information you can get on any school will come from students who are going or recently went there. These are the people who chose the place, paid the tuition, and did or are doing the time. More likely than not, they'll have a lot to say about the program and even the instructors.

Of course, when you visit a campus you can easily talk to the students. Just ask the program coordinator if they can connect you with some of them or you can go about it by waiting outside the classroom or building and just approaching some students yourself. In general, if you attend a formal information session on campus, the school will usually have some students there with whom you can speak. Just keep in mind that these students are often hand-picked by the administration and they may not be the most willing to tell you any downsides.

If you want to talk to some students before you even visit a campus because it's very far from where you live, try calling the program coordinator and just asking them if they can put you in touch with any students. Offer to provide your email so they can share it with students who are willing to reach out to you. You can then arrange a time to speak on the phone with them. If a school isn't willing to help you connect with current students or recent graduates, this may serve as a warning. In that case, it'll be up to you to decide for yourself if it's worth considering a school that doesn't encourage communication between potential students and the current student body or alumni.

#34: Talking to Instructors

Taking the time to talk to the people who will be a huge part of your studies shouldn't be overlooked. Your potential instructors are the most important people when it comes to the quality of education you're going to get at any school.

Formal information sessions and open house days will always have some instructors on hand to meet with potential students, so again, it's a good idea to attend them. If you can't attend because the school is too far away or the session just doesn't work with your schedule, then don't hesitate to call the school and ask for the contact information of their instructors (if it's not already listed on their website). You can even get the office hours of instructors and make appointments to go in and meet them in person.

In most cases, instructors are happy to talk or meet with potential students. If they aren't, this is another warning. Why wouldn't they be willing to take time to meet with you or have a chat on the phone? If they can't be bothered to help a potential student learn about the program, their teaching philosophy, or the school's facilities, how interested will they be in helping you learn once you're actually their student?

#35: Questions to Ask

By the time you've finished this book, you should have a really good idea of the kinds of questions you want to ask based on your own individual circumstances, needs and wants. But there are some key questions you'll want answered no matter who you are because the answers are critical for anyone wanting the best culinary education available to them.

Classroom size: How many students are in a class with you? In other words, what's the student to instructor ratio? Twenty students per instructor? Thirty? The smaller the class size the more attention each student gets.

Completion rate: How many students who enroll in the program actually complete it? A high drop-out rate can be an indication that a program either isn't great or that it's too expensive for the quality of education they offer.

Internships/Apprenticeships: Does the program require that students complete an intern/apprenticeship? Are they paid? How many hours are required? Does the school place students in an intern/apprenticeship? If not, will they help students to find one?

Career placement: What is the employment rate of graduates? Meaning, what percentage of students who complete the program find jobs in the industry upon graduation. Does the school have a career counseling office that does more than just tell you what websites list jobs? Do they actively help you to secure your first job? Do they help alumni with job placement even after their first job? Will the school always be a job placement resource for you into the future?

#36: Other Resources

There's no shortage of culinary school resources on the internet. From websites that simply offer lists of schools to Googling the names of schools, instructors, and alumni, to seeking out discussion forums frequented by culinary students, you can spend hours on end researching and comparing culinary schools on the web. Given that some schools have been sued by students who claim they were misled and duped, you may even want to Google the word "lawsuit" along with the name of the schools you're considering and see if anything pops up in the query results.

Other great resources are national, state, and local culinary and hospitality associations. The National Restaurant Association has chapters across the country as do seemingly countless other professional associations for everything from baking and pastry to hospitality, hotels, and wine. Make use of these resources, call the local chapters, ask them about the schools you're considering. Some of their members may be recent graduates of the programs you're considering. Professional associations are made up of just that, *professionals*, and they know the business way better than you do at this point, so make use of them!

Chef bios can also help you in your research. There's surely a chef (or a dozen chefs) whose work you admire. Find out where they went to school. Google them and see if any of the schools you're considering have graduated more than one of your culinary idols. You can also research how active these chefs might be on the campus, if they conduct visiting demonstrations or even if they give preference to interns and job seekers from their alma mater.

Emeril Lagasse, a graduate of Johnson & Wales who sits on its Board of Directors, told me in an interview, "I keep close ties with my alma mater. I go to the campus as often as I can, I help them with fundraising, and I do everything I can to add to the quality of education Johnson & Wales students are getting year after year."

CHAPTER 5

THE BEST SCHOOL FOR YOU

#37: Personal Preferences

So much about the decision to go to school and which school to go to depends on your own personal circumstances and preferences. What may be the best school for someone else may be the worst choice for you. In a meaningful way, thinking about and researching culinary programs can be a personal journey of getting to know yourself in a new light and thinking realistically about your present and future.

Nobody can tell you which school is your dream school, where it should be located, or what matters to you in a school. This is something you're just going to have to decide for yourself after taking all things into consideration. Although this is your own decision to make, talk to your friends and family. They know you, and they can help you to make the right decision based on the things they know are important to you.

#38: School Activities

From small, private, six-month programs to large, four-year college settings, nearly all culinary schools and programs offer extracurricular activities. What exactly they offer, however, can vary wildly from campus to campus.

Do you love any sports? Want to be on a collegiate athletic team? You're not going to get this from a devoted culinary school. Nor will you find things like orchestras or bands to join, plays and theatrical productions to get involved with, or sororities and fraternities. On the other hand, community colleges and four-year universities will have a large diversity of student activities; everything from a school newspaper, a skiing club, an equestrian program, foreign language and travel clubs, sports teams, chorus, band, and on and on. Colleges and universities can offer you an outlet for your other passions so if that's important to you, you might want to focus your research on schools that can give you a broader undergraduate experience.

You'll also want to look into what extracurricular, food-related activities are available to culinary students. Is the school involved in any local culinary festivals? Do the students have the opportunity to participate in culinary competitions? Is there a chapter of the American Culinary Federation or other culinary organization on campus? Does the school have a restaurant or bakery that is staffed by students? Do students have the opportunity to assist teachers in their extracurricular projects like cookbooks, demonstrations, or competitions?

When you start researching schools, you'll discover all kinds of activities in which you can participate and it will help you to think about what you want in your own school's extracurricular activities.

#39: Big Name Chefs

How important is it to go to a school that's graduated a lot of big names in the industry? In reality, it may not be as important as you think.

So much of what makes a great chef great is the work they do after school; the very hard work. Of course a great culinary program can make a huge difference at the beginning of your career and even beyond, but be cautious of choosing a program based solely on its alumni. There's no telling what changes the school has undergone since their time there—for better or for worse. Including the celebrity factor in your decision-making process can be useful, but it really shouldn't be the deciding factor. For all you know, that famous chef you admire so much might have hated the school they attended and their long-term success had nothing to do with it.

Schools with a lot of celebrity grads will definitely blow this horn as loudly as they can, just don't let it deafen you to all the other more important factors that go into making a school the right one for you.

What may matter for you in a potential program is how many big chefs come to the campus to conduct demonstrations and seminars. Some schools get a lot of great talent coming for guest lectures and others not so many. You may even want to know if your instructors have a big name in the industry, have published a lot of books or won competitions. But a big-name instructor may not equal a great teacher; it could mean they give teaching a lower priority than writing or competing!

#40: Go Local

Thankfully there are so many culinary programs all over America that for many of you, moving to a new town or city to get your education won't even be a part of your decision. Going to school where you're already living offers convenience, less hassle, more affordability, and perhaps the ability to save even more money by living with your parents, or staying put because you *are* a parent, and you don't want to leave or uproot your family.

When you live near even just one school that offers a culinary or pastry program, start by looking into this school first. If you love it and it's convenient, then be happy you got it so easy and look no further. Even if the school doesn't seem like your ideal, you may still want to consider attending and then relocating after graduation to get a job in the best kitchen that will have you. For so many reasons—financial and personal—not having to relocate to go to culinary school will make your life a lot easier.

#41: Relocate

If you live someplace where there just aren't any programs that are geographically convenient, then your burning desire to go to school will require you to relocate. Unfortunately for those wanting to study pastry arts, there are fewer programs in remote locations than there are culinary arts programs, so you might find you simply have to move.

Even if you don't have to, you may want to relocate for other reasons. Moving can be an adventure; it offers the excitement of a new life, new experiences, new people, and even a new culture if you choose to study abroad. Of her experience living in Paris to attend La Varenne, Tish Boyle said, "Just being in Paris, with all its phenomenal restaurants and food markets was an education in itself. Chefs from some of the best restaurants in France would come to the school frequently and give demos. In our free time, my friends and I would go on spontaneous field trips like spending a weekend at a foie gras farm in Perigord or mushroom picking in the Loire Valley. It was the experience of a lifetime, and one I never would have had at an American school."

#42: Rural Locations

There's always an assumption that the bigger the city, the more it has to offer someone pursuing a culinary education. While it's true that big cities have a lot to offer, and big city schools along with them, there are some things about rural life and education that no city can match.

If you want a culinary program that incorporates the farm-to-table movement and has its students working in the field as well as working in a kitchen, then a big city program won't work for you. Rural programs can have school farms where students learn how to grow organic crops, cook seasonally, and even humanely raise live-stock. You can even find culinary schools in rural settings that have or are associated with a vineyard. And then there's just the simple fact that some people prefer the serenity of a rural life to the chaos of a city life.

Oscar Ortega, Executive Pastry Chef/Owner of Atelier Ortega and ChocoLove in Jackson Hole, Wyoming, and a *Dessert Professional* 2011 Top Ten Pastry Chef in America, told me why he loves living off the beaten path. "I see myself as an artist," said Ortega, "and in order to create and to realize my vision, I need to live somewhere peaceful that I love. I just couldn't do what I do in a big city."

#43: City Locations

Undeniably, a major bonus to living in a big city for a culinary student is the restaurant scene. Even if you can't afford to eat at the top tables every night, you'll have the opportunity to work in their kitchens.

Christopher Schaefer, a graduate of the French Culinary Institute in New York City, relocated from Northern Virginia to study pastry arts. He would go to class in the morning and afternoon and then he would work (for free) at least three nights a week. He just walked into some of the best establishments in New York City, asked to talk to the pastry chef, and then asked if he could work for them without pay. Nobody said no and his experience in the pastry kitchens at restaurant Bouley under Alex Grunert, the Bouley Bakery under Damien Herrgott, and wd~50 under Sam Mason made relocating well worth the hassle and the cost for him.

City life also offers a vibrant culinary scene beyond restaurants. All year long you'll find culinary events, food festivals, industry trade shows, and other similar foodie goings-on that you can attend when you're not in class. Cities are also magnets for big-name chefs. They take their books on tour to cities, they make public appearances, and they're all over the event calendar. So you're going to have much more opportunity to see your favorite chef in person than you would outside a major city.

Just know this: living in a city will definitely cost you more than living in a rural part of the country and because there's always something going on, you'll be tempted to spend even more money than perhaps you should when you're a student.

#44: Age as a Factor

To figure out the kind of school that's going to be right for you, you might want to factor in your age. Though age doesn't matter with many things in life, when it comes to going to school, it can make a big difference in the program you choose.

If you're just out of high school and planning to attend a culinary program, you've got the most freedom. You're young so you shouldn't feel as if you're in any hurry to get your education over and done with as quickly as possible. You can take your time and attend a two-year program. You can even take the longer road and go for a bachelor's degree. Since the intensive, six-month programs will cost you more than a two-year program at a community college and as much as a bachelor's degree program at a university, expense may be more of a factor than time.

However, if you're not fresh out of high school or still in your twenties, then time may be of the essence. In this case, a full-time, intensive program may be your best option. It's not often that a thirty or forty-year-old wants to take the time to do a bachelor's degree or even an associate's.

But if you're willing to devote the time, then don't let your age restrict you. Figure out how you can make it work—people have and people do! You may even find that the flexibility of a two or four-year program works better for you because you can more easily find the time to still work and earn an income while you're in school.

#45: Consider Finances Realistically

One of the biggest mistakes you can make in planning your culinary education is to underestimate the importance of financial considerations. If your "dream school" costs $40,000 and you just can't afford that, then it could well end up your nightmare school. Perhaps your ideal school requires that you move, but you can't afford to relocate. In that case, maybe it isn't so ideal.

Don't ignore your personal financial situation. If you think you may have to borrow money in order to attend a more expensive, private program, do research into loans and loan payments. The truth is, you really won't earn more than minimum wage to a maximum of $12 an hour in your first job, even coming out of one of the best culinary programs in the country. So find out how much your monthly loan payments will be after graduation and then do the math.

Just don't bury your head in the sand when it comes to money. If you're willing to make financial sacrifices for your passion (as most of us are), then go ahead and make them. But make them knowing that you've calculated everything and you won't find yourself unpleasantly surprised.

CHAPTER 6

FINANCING CULINARY SCHOOL

#46: Significant Investment

Don't kid yourself. Depending on the program you choose, culinary school can be a huge investment. If you haven't thought things through and aren't 100 percent sure you want to pursue a career in the culinary industry, then it might end up being a huge waste of your money, time, and effort.

I've known people who thought they wanted to be a chef and borrowed tens of thousands of dollars to go to school, only to discover half-way through the program or in their first job that working in a kitchen wasn't what they wanted after all. When I asked Johnny Iuzzini what advice he would give to people considering going to culinary school, he said, "Go to work in a professional kitchen. See what it's *really* like, then decide if you want to work in this field. If you still want to, *then* you can decide if you want to go to culinary school."

If you just can't make the financial investment or don't want to, this doesn't mean your dream of a career in the culinary industry is dead. There's more than one way to reach the same goal, as I'll discuss later in Chapter 9.

#47: Student Loans

The vast majority of culinary programs, from six months to four years, qualify for their students to secure subsidized federal and state student loans. In most cases, you can borrow up to 100 percent of your tuition and payments on loans are deferred until you finish your program.

With the rising cost of culinary school, today more and more students are turning to government subsidized loans. So don't feel badly if you have to borrow money to go to school—most people do. Just don't be stupid about borrowing money. At the end of the day, debt is debt and it will have to be paid back. With a low-level starting salary, it won't be easy, but it can be done.

#48: Pitfalls of Loans

The youngest among you might not realize the importance of paying back your student loans, but don't make the mistake of learning the hard way. If you hurt your credit rating by defaulting on your loans, it can affect your ability to rent a good apartment, buy or lease a car, sometimes even get a job (yes, employers can and do run a credit check on you!).

So long as you dodge paying back your student loans, they will accrue interest and penalty fees will be added to the total every year. If you do the math, you'll see that for someone who borrows $30,000 to go to school and who then tries to avoid repayment for ten years, they can end up consequently owing $60,000 and that number will just keep growing.

No matter how much you may want to avoid repayment, you can't default on your student loans without it coming back to bite you!

#49: Grants

A lot of culinary schools, colleges, and universities offer government grants to financially qualifying students. By far the majority of grants are needs-based, so they're there for students who would have a difficult time paying for their education without them.

While federal and state governments have cut back on grant programs, they do still exist. If you do have a financial need, you should definitely apply for every grant you can. Grants won't usually cover your entire tuition, but they will help to lower the amount of money you need to borrow to go to school.

When you're researching schools, you'll definitely want to talk to someone at the school about financial aid. Some of the private, six-month programs don't qualify for government grants for students and this won't be a fact that they advertise. So ask them if they offer grants for qualifying students and don't be shy about it, it's just too important!

#50: Work/Study

Many colleges and universities offer a student work/study program, whereby students can earn a portion of their tuition by working in any number of on-campus jobs. How much you can work off in comparison to how much you must pay in tuition will of course vary from campus to campus, but it could be a great solution for you.

Make sure when you're looking into schools that you ask the financial aid counselor about work/study, and not just if the institution offers it. Ask them details about their work/study program. How much tuition credit is earned for every hour worked (equating credit to dollar amounts)? Figure out the credit as an hourly wage. If the work/study program isn't a great one, then you may be better off just getting a job and paying a portion of your tuition yourself. Generally, work/study programs do offer more than you could make with a regular job because the school appreciates the point of the program. Just don't take that for granted and assume you're getting a better deal with work/study.

You might also want to ask about the work options. If as a culinary student they have you working in the cafeteria, campus restaurant, or alumni and faculty club where they hold nice dinners and banquets, then this would be ideal. But if they have you doing a job that's far from your passion, it might not seem worthwhile to you unless the financial reward is great enough.

#51: Scholarships

Scholarships may be hard to come by, but thankfully for you, today there are more culinary scholarships available than at any point in the history of culinary school. The rising cost of education is being met with the rising number of successful chefs and hospitality professionals who want to give back.

Any good culinary program can guide you towards finding scholarships. Many have scholarships that are only available at their particular school, but all of them ought to be able to tell you about the scholarships that are available no matter where you study. If you're dealing with a culinary program coordinator who can't help you locate and apply for scholarships, this isn't such a good thing and you might want to think twice about going to that school.

The internet is a good place to research scholarships as are local chapters of the American Culinary Federation, the National Restaurant Association, and C-CAP. Get started on your research early so you can see what it takes to qualify for any number of scholarships and gather the necessary application materials. Often scholarships are based on achievement and not financial need, so you'll need good enough grades, letters of recommendation, and sometimes industry experience to qualify. Because they're highly competitive and come with strict qualifying criteria and deadlines, it's great to begin researching scholarships a full year before you'll have to start applying for them.

#52: Saving Up

Perhaps in the debt-heavy world in which we live today the notion of saving up for school seems outdated. Truth is, it shouldn't be.

You *can* take a year to work full time, even work a full-time job *and* a part-time job, and put away as much money as you possibly can—making sacrifices along the way—in order to be able to pay for your culinary education. Sure it wouldn't be easy, but the greatest among us make giant sacrifices to attain our dreams. It would be hard work and require discipline and patience, but then a career in the kitchen also takes hard work, discipline, and patience.

Saving for school, even starting to save when you're still in high school, could end up meaning you don't have to borrow any money at all and you'll definitely have to borrow less if you still need a student loan. Plus, you'll gain a sense of pride and satisfaction knowing you worked your tail off for it.

Of course, not everyone has the time in their lives to work and save patiently before beginning culinary school. Only you know this about yourself, so be honest with yourself about it.

#53: Working While Studying

You always have the option of working part time (or even full time) while you're in culinary school. You may still have to take out student loans, but if you work and save while going to school, you'll get a head start on paying off your loans.

There are other advantages to working while you're in school, especially when you consider you can always find a job in the culinary or hospitality industry. The pay in the back of the house won't be great, but you'll gain real experience and be ahead of the non-working competition when you graduate. If you finish school with a certificate, degree, or diploma *and* job experience, you'll not only be better off financially, you'll be more competitive in the job market.

It's also worth exploring a front-of-the-house position as a server or even a runner in a high-end restaurant. While this won't teach you cooking or baking skills, it will give you a broader understanding of the whole operation and you can make better money when tips are involved. Plus, it can be relatively easy to find flexible part-time positions in the front of the house that will make it easier for you to hold a job while you're in school.

Of course, if you've already got a higher income than you would earn in foodservice or through work/study, even if the work is unrelated to cooking, then consider keeping your job and maybe cutting back to part time or going freelance. If you can earn as much in a few hours at your current job as you would in a whole day of kitchen work, it's up to you to decide what's more important given your personal circumstances.

#54: Paying Off Debt

However much money you borrow for school, you don't want to end up like the group of 8,500 culinary students from the California Culinary Academy that I mentioned in my introduction. Whether or not it was their fault to take out such large loans and consequently wind up unable to repay them, there's always a degree of personal responsibility that nobody can deny. Even considering the deceptive practices of the school, the students could have done better research; the kind of research I'm encouraging you to do.

Paying off debt is *not* going to be easy after you graduate from culinary school. You will *not* get a high paying job right after graduation unless you have some family-run business that will let you jump way up the ladder on day one. Still, paying off your debt doesn't have to be as painful as it seems to have been for the students involved in the lawsuit.

Sadly a little known fact, the Department of Education does offer options for lower income workers saddled with student loans. These plans are called Extended Repayment, Graduated Repayment, Income Contingent Repayment, and Income-Based Repayment. Each of these repayment programs offers different ways to make paying off your student loans not only less painful, but just plain do-able. And the information about these plans is easy to find on the Department of Education's website.

CHAPTER 7

MAKING THE MOST OF SCHOOL

#55: Go Beyond the Classroom

In today's cut-throat culinary industry, even completing a top notch program may not give you the upper hand when it's time to go job hunting. If you're not going to a well-known culinary school, it can be even more important to do more than just attend your classes and complete your projects.

If you want to get ahead of the competition before you even graduate, you'll want to extend yourself into areas beyond the classroom. This will not only give you more experience, connections, and potential references, it'll give you more inspiration and motivation for practicing your craft.

#56: Be Active On Campus

Get to know your school's campus and all it has to offer culinary students and then get involved. You might also want to see what activities interest you that aren't specifically for culinary students. Having other interests and pursuing them can give you some interesting, conversation-starting additions to your résumé.

If you're on a campus that doesn't offer a whole lot of activities for culinary students, consider starting some yourself and getting other students involved. Maybe you want to start a student newsletter or blog, a dinner or recipe club, or organize outings to places like organic farms, vineyards, or large production bakeries. Perhaps you can reach out to some successful chefs and invite them to come do a demo at your school.

Taking the initiative to start something new on your campus that all culinary students can get involved with will show how passionate and motivated you are, and it'll show that you can assume a leadership role and utilize organizational skills—all of which look great on a résumé!

#57: Volunteer Off Campus

All over the country, you'll find culinary events, food festivals, and even non-profit organizations that need volunteers who can lend a culinary hand. Getting involved in volunteer work can expose you to chefs, industry insiders, and culinary trends.

Today's chefs are more socially conscious than ever before. Whether they're involved in the big, national hunger-relief efforts like Share Our Strength or The Great American Bake Sale, or culinary education organizations like C-CAP, chefs are doing more than ever before.

To name just a few, Bobby Flay told me of his work with organizations that rescue Thoroughbred ex-racehorses and Duff Goldman explained his involvement with the local Girls Club in the Lower East Side of Manhattan (they have their own bakery!). Emeril Lagasse talked with me very passionately about his life-long charity involvement and his own Emeril Lagasse Foundation, and Marcus Samuelsson spoke with me of his dedication to C-CAP.

Volunteering with a charity or culinary event while you're still in school will look great on your résumé, will show your prospective employers that you care, *and* will do some good for the world too!

#58: Culinary Student Organizations

If you choose a school that has a lot of student clubs, don't overlook them. Dive in! Depending on the school you choose, you might find student chapters of SkillsUSA, the American Culinary Federation, The National Restaurant Association, The Bread Bakers Guild of America, Women Chefs & Restaurateurs, and so many more. The benefits of joining these kinds of organizations can't be underestimated. They will open doors of opportunity for you that can take you places you might not go without them.

If the school you really want to attend doesn't have any culinary student organizations that are affiliated with a national or state professional group, then you can always take the initiative and look into starting a chapter yourself. If you contact the national or state headquarters of any culinary organization, they'll likely be more than happy to help you.

#59: Build Relationships with Instructors

I can't stress how important it is to really get to know your instructors and let them get to know you. You don't have to be the teacher's pet, but you shouldn't be just a name on the roster to them either.

Coming out of culinary school and looking for your first position, you'll want letters of recommendation from your instructors. If they have a deeper relationship with you beyond just being another face in the classroom and kitchen, chances are you'll get a better letter from them.

Pay attention to your instructors' office hours and go visit them. That's your best opportunity to spend one-on-one time with them. Ask questions about what you're learning, about the industry, about their own background and experiences in the field. Your instructors have more to teach you than just your daily lessons; they have life and career lessons to pass on as well and any good instructor will be happy to share their wisdom with you. Your instructors can become your mentors when they get to know you and the relationship you develop with them can last throughout your career.

#60: Read More

Culinary school always comes with textbooks, but why stop there? Take the time to bury your nose in great cookbooks, magazines, and even chef memoirs.

No culinary student bookshelf should be without *Larousse Gastronomy*. A whopping huge hardback, it's literally the encyclopedia of cooking. Another great book is *Complete Techniques* by Jacques Pèpin. Rose Levy Beranbaum has some amazing "Bibles" for bakers, so if you're doing pastry, be sure to grab her books too. And no cookie aficionado should be without Tish Boyle's *The Good Cookie*. Thanks to online retailers, you can find decent used copies on all these great books without having to spend a fortune.

Dessert Professional magazine is a wonderful resource for budding pastry chefs, and on the savory side there's no substitute for *Art Culinaire*. Some other great magazines are *Fine Cooking* and *Cook's Illustrated*, both of which have way more in-depth cooking content than irrelevant advertising. You can also check out industry trade magazines like *Nation's*

Restaurant News which sometimes offer student discounts on subscriptions.

#61: Compete

There's no shortage of student culinary and pastry competitions across America, so you shouldn't have too hard a time finding one in which you can participate. The American Culinary Federation, SkillsUSA, and others are always holding competitions for student teams.

If competition is important to you, ask the schools you're considering if they have teams that compete at any level. If they don't, ask if they'd be open to you organizing a team yourself. Outside of just the student competition setting, you can also look for cooking, baking, and recipe competitions that are open to the public, no matter what your culinary background.

Kerry Vincent, judge on *Food Network Challenge* and *Last Cake Standing* and founder of the Oklahoma State Sugar Arts Show, has a long history on the competition circuit and hundreds of blue ribbons to show for it. She told me why she thinks competition is so important. "When you compete, you get the chance to push yourself beyond your limits," she said.

"Competition tests your organizational skills, your ability to perform under pressure, and your quick thinking and reflexes. It'll toughen you up too! And when you pay attention to the work of the other competitors, you can learn so much from them that even when you don't win, you still come out ahead."

#62: Attend Industry Events

Every year in New York City, StarChefs.com organizes one of the best culinary industry events in America. The StarChefs.com International Chefs Congress is an industry-only event that gathers the world's top savory, pastry, wine, and mixology talent and brings them together for three days of demonstrations, seminars, workshops, and networking. Culinary students are welcome at the StarChefs.com ICC and their website even has a page where you can look for a couch to crash on if you're traveling from out of town.

Other great events are All Things Baking in Chicago, The International Baking Industry Expo in Las Vegas, The Winter Fancy Food Show in San Francisco, The Amoretti National Pastry Team Championships & International

Pastry Forum, and The International Association of Culinary Professionals Annual Conference. But that's just the tip of the industry event iceberg!

Attending culinary industry events will fill you with knowledge and inspiration and give you the indispensible opportunity to network with people from across the country and the world.

#63: Work for Free

Whether or not you're working for pay, you might want to consider working even just one shift per week for free when you're a student. While it's going to be tough to get a paying job in a Michelin-starred kitchen while you're still a student, you'd be surprised how open any acclaimed kitchen can be to having you if you're willing to work for free.

Just gather the courage to walk into any fine dining restaurant, high end patisserie, hotel, chocolate shop, or whatever applies to your particular interests and tell them you're looking to get some experience working for free in their kitchen. Just don't show up during crunch time or nobody will be able to talk to you and it'll seem like you don't have an appreciation for how busy they are.

Once you land a free gig, treat it with the respect you would a paying position. Show up when you say you're going to be there, don't pull any disappearing acts, and work your butt off doing whatever they need you to do. If you can't take it seriously and perform your personal best, you'll end up doing your reputation more harm than good!

CHAPTER 8

WHAT TO EXPECT AFTER GRADUATION

#64: Not a Chef Yet

When you've finally finished your culinary program, especially if was long or expensive, don't fall into the trap of thinking you're now a chef. Sorry to say, nobody coming straight out of culinary school is a chef just yet, so don't cop that attitude.

Yes, you want to project confidence in the skills you've learned, what you've accomplished, and all of the things you've done while in school, but confidence is not the same thing as expecting a chef-level salary or acting like a know-it-all. And there are few things that bother head chefs more than upstarts who think they know everything.

It takes years of experience, moving up the culinary ladder rung by rung, until you'll earn the title of chef or pastry chef, let alone executive chef or executive pastry chef. In an interview with Susur Lee, acclaimed Chef/Owner of several restaurants around the world and a finalist on *Top Chef Masters*, he told me his impressions about starting out. "You've got to work for at least ten years to understand things like slow cooking, timing, patience, and the stages of preparation. Learning all of what I call the 'little big things,' working double time to become good, is really intense. But you have to do it all before you can earn the title of chef. Too many people in this generation don't want to work so hard and it can make them impatient, unfocused, and frustrated."

#65: Crafting Your Résumé

Before you start your job search, make sure you've got a killer résumé ready to go. Of course you'll include your education in your résumé and your grades if you went to a school that had a grading system, but you'll also want to include other important information.

If you followed the advice in this book and made the most of your time in school, getting involved in culinary clubs, participating in competitions, volunteering, and all the rest, then all of this goes into your résumé. If you competed but didn't win, include it. This shows your high level of motivation and dedication.

You'll also want to gather some letters of recommendation to attach to your résumé. Teachers, employers (culinary or otherwise), and people for whom you volunteered are all great sources for letters of recommendation. Just remember to do your best all along the way so when it's time to ask for letters of recommendation you actually get good ones!

Make your résumé sharp. It sounds simple, but it's too often overlooked. Even if you're not the world's best speller or writer, you just can't hand out résumés with bad grammar, type errors, or misspelled words. Run spell check and ask someone to proofread your résumé for you. Just don't run with a draft résumé that hasn't been proofed and polished. It'll look sloppy, and nobody wants to hire a sloppy kitchen worker!

#66: Looking for Work

One of the biggest go-to sources for culinary jobs is Craigslist. With a Craigslist site for pretty much every city and town in America, you can search in your area or expand nationally. More and more chefs turn to Craigslist to run ads and for this reason alone it's a great resource for job hunting.

Other good resources for culinary jobs are the Job Finder on StarChefs.com, and the websites CulinaryCrossing and HospitalityCrossing. You can also directly target specific employers who are large enough to include current positions on their websites; places like hotels as well as large restaurant groups like Jean-Georges list career opportunities.

You can also do leg-work by going door to door and walking right into the establishments where you'd love to work. Dress professionally, bring copies of your résumé and letters of recommendation to leave with the chef, and never, ever walk in during busy service. If you go when it's a slow time of day, you may even get to meet with the chef right on the spot.

#67: Use Your Connections

If you've made the most of school, then you've built up a network of connections within the culinary and hospitality industry. Even if you don't think you have a large network, each individual connection you have has their own network they can tap into on your behalf.

Ask around to see if anyone you know is aware of any positions. A lot of times when a chef knows someone is leaving their kitchen, they'll look to the people they know before they run an ad. If you can merge into this inside track, then you're ahead in the race and that's the whole point of having connections.

Just remember that your connections will only be as willing to recommend you as you were willing to work hard and show them your best. You can know tons of people, but if they all know you as a slacker who never took school or work seriously, well then obviously they won't be all that willing to help you find a job. Also, when someone recommends you, their name is on the line. You'll want to do your best if you land a job through a connection or they'll never help you again.

#68: Internships

Sometimes, if your school didn't require an internship (or if it wasn't a very long one), then you may find it easier to secure an internship right out of school instead of a job.

While many internships don't pay anything, others might pay less than minimum wage, but at least it's something. You'll likely have a better chance of landing in a prestigious kitchen and working and learning from the best chefs right out of school if you get your foot in the door as an intern.

If this is financially do-able for you, then be sure to tell prospective employers that you're willing to take an internship position and expand your search to include not only entry-level jobs, but internships as well. And remember, if you do well and prove your worth as an intern, you may even get offered a real position when one opens up.

#69: Grunt Work

Even when you land a paid position, go into it knowing that on the entry-level rung, you're going to be doing grunt work, and a lot of it. In reality, there's not a huge difference between the work you'll be doing as an intern versus being a paid employee. Either way, you're still at the bottom of the food chain.

You're going to peel seven-hundred potatoes, segment five boxes of oranges, separate dozens of eggs, lift and carry huge sacks of flour, pluck pigeons and chickens, and chop hundreds of onions. And that's just the beginning. Your work is going to seem mundane, redundant, and boring. You're going to wonder why you bothered going to school when all they have you doing is grunt work.

The answer is that every chef started out doing exactly what you're going to be doing. How do you think they can peel so quickly and efficiently? Chop so accurately with lightening speed? Separate eggs without breaking a single yolk? Because they've done it a million times!

Like Emeril Lagasse said to me, "There is no easy or quick way if you want to be successful and do things right. There's no cutting corners. It just takes time and it takes hard work to become a chef."

#70: Kitchen Realities

Unlike a school kitchen, a real kitchen is a crazy, insane place to be. It's hot, steamy, loud, slippery, fast-paced, hectic, dangerous, crass, and unsympathetic. But for lovers of the job, it's also home.

When I asked him what he would say to people going into their first job in a kitchen, Duff Goldman said, "The environment is not easy and it's not conducive to the frail. It's tough. You've got to be prepared for the rigors of standing on your feet for fifteen hours while someone is yelling at you!"

You've also got to be prepared for practical jokes and pranks. Pastry Chef Damien Herrgott told me that in Paris, his team would send all interns out on an errand to go and buy some "powdered water" because they had run out. Amazingly, nearly all interns and new hires would say "yes chef!" and go out earnestly looking for powdered water. No, there's no such thing. But, Herrgott said, "One intern did come back with regular water, saying it was 'reconstituted powdered water,' the shop was in on the joke!"

Sometimes the jokes can get even more embarrassing. You may get your pants pulled down, your shirt pulled up, your clothes might disappear from your locker, or you may get locked in the walk-in. Whatever they throw your way, don't take it personally. Laugh, don't cry or get offended, because practical jokes are a character builder and they're also what make you part of the family!

#71: Working Your Butt Off

Being the new hire or the intern, you're going to want to keep your head down, your mouth shut, and your hands busy. However much work they give you, however long you're standing up, bending over, developing calluses on your hands, cutting and burning yourself, and sweating it out, *do not complain!*

Nothing impresses a chef less than a new hire who can't hack it. Every chef started where you are and every great chef worked their butt off. What will get you noticed and ahead will be your work ethic, stamina, and drive.

The public image of what it's like to be a chef is very far removed from the real blood, sweat, and tears that chefs live through every day. This public perception doesn't include busting your ass in what's actually not a very glamorous job. Shuna Lydon, Executive Pastry Chef of Peels NYC, told me this about the stark contrast between the real hard work of a chef and the image created by the media: "What's shown to the general public about our work is hi-gloss, perfect smiles, upper-class spreads of perfect food in a beautiful windowsill and our chefs in designer dresses and shoes schmoozing at gorgeous ranches in Colorado. It's so far from our day to day it would be like creating a hospital show where no one gets hurt!"

#72: Travel to the Top

One of the most advantageous things a culinary school grad can do is travel to work overseas. If your goal is to be a world-class pastry chef, why not go to France and intern there? If your goal is to become an Italian savory chef, a master of pizza or pasta, where better to learn than in Italy? Most American chefs who specialize in a foreign cuisine have spent a lot of time actually working in countries where what was foreign to them was native to the chef under whom they worked.

Roy Shvartzapel, a grad of the CIA, used his connections, specifically his mentor Damien Herrgott, to land internships at both Pierre Hermé in Paris and elBulli in Spain. They didn't pay him, but having these world-class establishments on his résumé made his rise to the top a hell of a lot quicker than most of his contemporaries. Just four years out of school, he was already the executive pastry chef at a Michelin two-star restaurant.

You may not have the funding to go straight from school to France or Italy to do an internship, but if you really want to go, it's worth saving up enough money to make it happen. Not only will you learn from the best sources of knowledge, you'll gain a life experience that's virtually second to none.

CHAPTER 9

ALTERNATIVES TO FULL-TIME EDUCATION

#73: School Isn't for Everyone

Whether it's because of time, money, or just your personality, school isn't for everyone. Luckily, a stellar career in the kitchen doesn't necessarily require going to school. While it'll likely be more difficult to land your first paid position without a culinary degree, diploma or certificate, it's certainly not impossible.

Chef-Owner Cesar Ramirez of the Michelin three-star Chef's Table at Brooklyn Fare didn't go to culinary school and yet today he's recognized as one of the top chefs in the world. Of his background Ramirez told me, "I hated school and I only went into a kitchen job because I needed a job, any job, if I was going to go out on my own and not go to college. But I loved the kitchen from the first day!"

#74: Apprenticeships

While doing an apprenticeship is a good idea for culinary school grads, it's almost an imperative if you want to skip school. Even if your schedule only allows apprenticing one or two days a week or weekend in a kitchen so you can keep your income-paying job, do it.

The important thing when doing an apprenticeship without any previous culinary training is to be honest about your background, be wide open to learning from your peers, and try to get into the best possible establishments that are also relevant to the kind of culinary career you want to build.

Susur Lee, who didn't go to culinary school but rather started work at age fifteen, told me about his experience as an apprentice. "Being an apprentice means finding yourself, discovering who you are in the kitchen. You're at the bottom and you have to show respect; and whatever they tell you to do, you do it without complaining. It can be mentally abusive, but it makes you grow up fast!"

#75: The Self-Taught Chef

Yes, there are self-taught chefs; people who learned to cook, bake, or decorate at home, reading everything they could get their hands on, and practicing hours on end.

World-renowned cake decorator Kerry Vincent didn't attend any pastry arts program. When she discovered her passion for cake decorating, she told me she began by buying tons of books and trailing pastry chefs in European kitchens. Then, when she started getting orders for cakes she'd never done before, she said, "I literally put my elbows on the counter of a baking supply shop with the manager who showed me how to make gum paste roses. Then I went home and practiced like crazy!"

If you want to teach yourself, you will still need the help of others. You'll find that help in books and magazines, you'll find it online, in kitchen trails, at demonstrations, and even at a supply store. Being self-taught doesn't mean being completely isolated.

#76: Part Time Education

If you do want a formal culinary education but the five-day-a-week, full-time program just isn't going to work for you, consider going part time.

Many programs, especially at community colleges and vocational-technical centers, offer the flexibility to attend class part time. It will take you longer to complete your degree or diploma, but you'll be able to maintain whatever full time job you have that pays the bills while steadily working your way towards graduation.

You'll find there are culinary programs, both private and public, that offer weekend and evening classes so it's a lot easier to complete the program without drastically altering the life you've already got going. So if you know that full-time schooling won't work for you, but you still want a culinary education, don't give up, find a part time program.

#77: Extension Classes

So many culinary schools and programs offer extension courses in very specific areas. Extension classes aren't free and often aren't cheap, but they run from one to three days and up to two weeks and are usually held on evenings and weekends.

Community and occupational centers offer these kinds of focused classes as do private schools like the Institute of Culinary Education, where they offer classes on a huge array of savory concentrations. The French Pastry School of Kennedy-King College, The Notter School of Pastry Arts, and the Barry Callebaut Chocolate Academy all offer extension classes. Even industry companies get in on the action, like the Five Star Pastry Series by PreGel.

Combining extension classes with self-teaching or even an apprenticeship will help you to hone your skills in specific areas and make new connections, plus they look great on a résumé.

#78: Trailing

If you're really green, not even a sprout but a seed, then you might want to consider trailing some people in their work. When you trail, you're not actually participating in the work of the kitchen, you're simply following someone around as they work and observing what they do. You won't ever get paid to trail, but you will get the chance to watch professionals at work. In a trail, you'll learn by watching and whether it's cooking, baking, decorating, or working with chocolate, there's a lot you can pick up just by observing.

When you trail, you stay out of the way. Before you start, find out if it's ok to ask questions while the person is at work or if it's better to make a note of your questions and ask them when the person's shift is over. Be quiet and courteous on a trail; remember you're not there to contribute. But, if you're asked if you want to contribute, don't hesitate, just do it. Trails can lead to internships, which can in turn lead to a job.

Landing a trail takes some foot work and you can go about finding a kitchen trail the same way I recommend looking for unpaid positions in #63.

#79: Seminars, Events & Demos

If you're not going to school, it's really worth it to check around for culinary seminars, events, and demonstrations and to attend as many as possible. All across the country, notable chefs make public appearances, conducting educational seminars and cooking demonstrations in places as diverse as cooking and baking supply retailers (Sur La Table and Williams-Sonoma), department stores (Macy's), schools, and food festivals.

To get beyond well-publicized food events, you may have to do some digging by searching the internet and making calls to find opportunities where you can watch the pros at work, ask them questions, and walk away with more knowledge than you had before. You won't get any credit for attending, but you will expose yourself to the work of professionals and some of the important lessons they have to teach, and you will find inspiration.

#80: Get a Job, ANY Job

When you feel you're ready to try for a job in a professional kitchen, you may not have the choice of being picky if you didn't go to culinary school. And really, any job will do at that point. Well-known and respected chefs have started their careers flipping burgers at McDonalds, making pizzas at Dominos, or baking cakes at the local supermarket. While they didn't plan to stay put indefinitely, these less-than-ideal jobs got their feet in the door.

What's important with your first job isn't the pay or prestige, it's the practical experience. Doing prep work, keeping your station clean, performing under heat and pressure, and working in a team are all things you just can't do when you're schooling yourself at home. And they're all things you'll need to know in order to get beyond the fast food kitchen or supermarket bakery. Bottom line is, these kinds of jobs will give you something real to put on your résumé so you can eventually go out and find better work.

So don't look at these kinds of jobs as beneath you. They can and will be an important stepping stone in your career. One day you'll look back on them with a smile and a sense of accomplishment, knowing how far you've come.

#81: Where to Land Work

Some of the best places to turn when you're first looking for a trail, internship, or job (whether or not you went to school) is to check with the establishments you've frequented as a customer. The restaurants where your family always eats, the hotels where they stay, or the local market where you and your family always shop are great starting points.

If you chose not to go to culinary school you may not have had the opportunity to build up a network of professional connections, so turn to your personal connections instead. Make a list of all the places you've frequented over the years and then start making the rounds. Explain to the managers of the foodservice establishments that know you as a customer that you're actually looking for work in a kitchen. Talk to them about your passion, how you want to work hard and learn from others. You're likely going to get a better reception from people who already know you than from people who don't and they'll be more willing to give you your first shot.

CHAPTER 10

FOR CAREER CHANGERS

#82: Special Considerations

There's a big difference between attending a culinary program when you're just out of high school (or still young enough to have not yet established a career in a different field) and attending culinary school when you've already dedicated ten, fifteen, or more years to another occupation. If you're a career changer, the decision to go to culinary school can be an even more difficult one to make, so you're going to have some special considerations to weigh to ensure you're making the right choice for you.

More than what I talk about in this chapter, you'll have a list of your own special considerations, and maybe even a few thrown in by your wife or husband, boyfriend or girlfriend, and perhaps even your kids. Pay attention to all of them. For the more mature among you, the decision to go to culinary school and switch career tracks well into your life journey should not be made in haste or isolation.

#83: Why Change Careers?

This may seem like a simple question, but it's not. Ask yourself why you want to change your career, go back to school, and start over at the bottom in a new field. Do you just hate your current job or boss? Do you have a passion for food and love cooking or baking in your free time? Does everyone tell you how talented you are and that you should go to culinary school? Really delve into the reasons behind this desire.

Truth is, you can change jobs within your established occupation and this might breathe new life into your current career. Cooking for friends and family, however many and however often, is nowhere near the same thing as working twelve-plus hours a day in a professional kitchen serving an untold number of covers and waiting years until you can actually create a menu yourself. There's a lot more to being a chef than making a nice meal or baking a great cake at home and potentially a lot less money in it than your current career. So ask yourself, really interrogate yourself, before you make such a huge, life-changing leap.

Like Duff Goldman said to me, "If you really like to cook at home, does that *really* mean you want to cook the exact same dish fifty times in one night without getting a break?"

#84: Sacrificing Income

Don't take this for granted, if you enroll in a culinary program, you will be sacrificing your current income, an income that's taken you years to attain. And you won't just be sacrificing income while you're a student. Once you're out of school, you'll be looking at a minimum wage income, if you're lucky, maybe you'll land a job that pays $10 or $12 per hour.

That's the reality, no matter what any school tells you about your immediate job prospects, you won't earn more than about $12 an hour. Think about that. Compare it to your current income.

Then, do a detailed accounting of all your expenses, and I mean ALL of them, for the past year of your life. Can you pay all of those expenses on a minimum wage salary? You can also look carefully at your expenses and see what you can realistically sacrifice. Try to figure out just what is the maximum you can cut from your budget, and then see if this can be covered with minimum wage earnings.

Just know for a fact that unless you're currently earning minimum wage, your income is going to take a hit, both during and after school, maybe even for years to come.

#85: Taking On Debt & Depleting Savings

Unless you have enough money saved up, chances are you're going to take on some debt to attend culinary school. Maybe you'll take out student loans, perhaps your credit card debt will increase, or you may have the ability to tap into the equity in your home or your retirement saving and use that kind of financing for tuition and expenses.

As I talked about earlier, today's culinary programs can cost a small fortune, and the majority of students do have to borrow to cover it. This becomes more significant, and maybe even more daunting, when you're thinking of changing careers. The financial one-two punch of losing income and taking on debt or depleting savings when you may be in a place right now where you're financially comfortable, deserves a long, hard look.

Your potential debt also warrants a serious discussion with your partner if you have one, and even your kids if you have any. Big changes to a family's debt or savings can hurt everyone, so don't ignore the input of everyone who will be affected by your decision.

#86: Program Length

Most of the career changers I know chose to enroll in a six-month intensive program rather than taking the time to complete a two or four-year program. Obviously this makes sense, if you're thirty or forty, the thought of spending that much of your life back in school before going out and building your new career may leave you disheartened.

The obvious advantage of an intensive program is speed, the obvious disadvantage is cost—these programs *will* make a bigger dent in your budget, some of them by a long way.

If you're fine with that, and time is more important to you than financial considerations, then go for it. Otherwise, you can choose a culinary program that offers evening and weekend classes, one you can attend part time, thus giving yourself the ability to maintain your current career and income—even on a part time or freelance basis—until you've completed school.

#87: In the Classroom

Most culinary schools and programs are full of young people ranging in age from about 18 to 26. If you're 36 or even 46, the thought of being the "oldest person in class" might turn you off the idea of school altogether. So you might want to do some extra research into finding a program that somehow caters to career changers and has a more mature student body.

Another thing to appreciate is that after having worked your way up the ladder in your current field, earning more responsibility and respect, it will take you down a peg (or ten) to find yourself in a classroom where you're granted the same amount of respect and responsibility as people nearly half your age.

Both of these considerations are true for any mature person returning to school—or attending school for the first time. While these are important things to think about, they definitely shouldn't stop you from pursuing your dream, and they shouldn't be the tipping point in making your decision. If after considering everything I've discussed in this book, and talking it all over with the people who will be most effected by your decision, you choose to go to culinary school, then forget about your age, enjoy it, and give it your all!

#88: A Master Plan

When I spoke with Richard Ruskell, Executive Pastry Chef of Montage Hotels, winner of *Food Network's Last Cake Standing*, and a career changer, about what it was like for him to go back to school in his thirties and start out at the bottom, he told me he had a master plan.

"I wasn't about to work an hourly, minimum wage job for years," said Ruskell, "so I planned to work as much as I could in the best kitchens that would have me, using my maturity to my advantage. I really hustled, I did a lot of competitions and worked my way up and into salaried, management-levels positions as quickly as possible."

Ruskell worked, competed, networked, and hustled his way to the top in just a few years because he had a plan. He chose a six-month, intensive pastry program, and he charted a course for his new career. Having your own plan may involve different choices than Ruskell's, the imperative thing for career changers is to have a plan that takes into account the time pressure you're likely to feel when you're just coming out of culinary school.

#89: Other Ways to Feed Your Passion

Having a passion for food doesn't necessitate that you go to culinary school and change careers. If you're already fulfilling your passion by being an avid and appreciated home cook or baker, you can always add to your skills by taking extension classes, going on culinary-focused vacations, and expanding your creativity. You might also be able to take your current career and apply it to the foodservice industry, thereby becoming involved with food at the professional level without having to go to culinary school.

The culinary and hospitality industry is serviced by all kinds of professionals who cater to their specific needs. Graphic designers, web-builders, HR, PR, marketing and communications professionals, architects, writers, engineers, interior designers, sales people, accountants, attorneys, event planners, and so many more can all gear their services specifically to chefs, restaurants, bakeries, hotels, you name it. Like Bobby Flay told me, "Opportunities are abundant in the culinary industry today. So you don't have to just be a chef."

#90: Everyone On Board

With career changers, often the choice to go to culinary school—as well as the more fundamental choice to change your career—is going to involve your family. Not your parents, but rather your spouse, your significant other, your kids—people who currently rely to some extent on your current income and the time you devote to them, people who are used to your—and their—lifestyle.

The sacrifices in time and money you'll have to make to go to school and then move into an incredibly challenging industry won't just be your own; they'll be sacrifices your whole family will have to make along with you. Your new career will come with a low starting income, back-breaking work, and totally irregular work schedules too. Weekends, nights and even holidays will no longer be dedicated to your family and friends; they'll be devoted to work.

So involve everyone in your decision-making process. Talk to them about all of your considerations, crunch the numbers with them, and make it clear to everyone just how much this will change all of your lives. You can even share this book with them so they also have a clear idea of what your choices involve. To succeed in school you're going to need their support and the best way to have it is to truly involve them in making these decisions.

CHAPTER 11

CREATING A
CULINARY CAREER

#91: The Reality of Success

In today's get-rich-quick, reality-TV world, the truth about what it's going to take to become a successful chef can seem harsh. There aren't any shortcuts and overnight success is a mirage for the meek.

With the dawn of shows like *Top Chef* and *The Next Food Network Star* coupled with twenty-something-year-old billionaires in the tech industry, it's not just beginning cooks who don't want to work long and hard to make it big, it's a lot of people in a lot of professions. Being a chef is damn hard work, there's no two ways about it.

When I asked Derek Emerson, three-time James Beard Award nominee and Chef/Owner of two of the most celebrated restaurants in Mississippi, why he went to culinary school, he replied, "I went to culinary school because I thought being a chef was going to be easy. Damn, was I sure wrong about that. Being a chef is a bitch!"

Success as a chef, even stardom, has to be earned the hard way. For every celebrity chef you hear about, every best-selling cookbook you read, every kitchen product launched by a chef, there's years and years of sweat equity behind them. No chef arrives at success by just dreaming about it and you won't either. Accept this as a fact. Don't complain about how long it's taking to get ahead and don't compare yourself to people who have years more experience than you. Just focus on yourself, your work, and doing the best you can do.

#92: The Truth Is Not Televised

Though I absolutely love it for entertainment, food television hasn't really done budding chefs a lot of favors. In the face of so much fame, too many people starting out in kitchens today just want to jump from culinary school on to a TV set. The fact that this giant leap has actually happened for a teaspoon-full of people only makes this unrealistic expectation all the more frustrating for 99.999 percent of today's kitchen neophytes.

Ace of Cakes Duff Goldman told me, "If anyone is thinking about going to culinary school *only* because they watch a lot of food TV, think it's cool, so they want to do what they're seeing, then they shouldn't go. What you see on TV isn't real, it's not what your life or career is really going to be like!"

When I was speaking with Bobby Flay about his television success, he reminded me of how many years he spent and how hard he slaved in a kitchen before ever appearing on TV. His advice for people who genuinely want a TV career? "Go to culinary school, spend years working in a real kitchen, and take some acting classes. Being a chef and being on TV are very different things, and while you have to be a chef first, it's not going to teach you how to perform in front of a camera." On the same topic, Emeril Lagasse told me, "I try to explain to people that just because you've graduated from culinary school, you're not going to walk straight on to the *Food Network* and have your own cooking show!"

#93: Personal Sacrifice

Know this: the life of a chef requires a great deal of personal sacrifice to attain professional success. While any burning ambition can be all consuming, the ambition of a chef can really take a toll on your personal life and relationships even more than other careers.

You work long hours (standing up and bending over), odd hours, either starting at 4 a.m. or working until 2 a.m. You have to work holidays and weekends, New Year's Eve and Day, Christmas, and Thanksgiving. Basically, you work when everyone else you know isn't working. Then, when you're not working, you can want nothing more than to just flop on the couch and spend your one day off being lazy and ordering take-out. And often the only time you can socialize is after work, going out late and staying out all night with your co-workers.

All of this usually doesn't go over well with boyfriends, girlfriends, wives, and husbands, let alone kids, so chefs have one of the highest divorce rates in the country. As Susur Lee said,

"Don't have a relationship for your first five years in a kitchen!"

#94: Professional Associations

One thing's for sure: there's no shortage of professional associations to join. The American Culinary Federation, Women Chefs & Restaurateurs, James Beard Foundation, The Bread Bakers Guild of America, The American Institute of Baking, The International Association of Culinary Professionals, and on it goes.

Joining a professional association can do your career a world of good. Not only do they provide ample networking opportunities, they'll also keep you up on industry news and trends, give you chances to attend conferences and meetings, and just keep you in the loop and active in your field.

The benefits of being a part of an industry association far outweigh the cost of membership. But you don't just want to be a member; you need to be an active member, so do your research. With so many organizations to choose from, and not enough time to be an active member in all of them, you'll want to choose your affiliations carefully so you can make the most of them.

#95: Trade Shows

I love culinary industry trade shows. They're huge gatherings of industry professionals and products and in the space of one to three days, you can meet so many people and learn about so many things going on in the culinary world today.

Most industry trade shows, like The International Restaurant & Foodservice Show of New York, also hold competitions so you can see the cutting edge work of up-and-coming chefs and pastry chefs. You can apply to compete yourself or just go to watch the competition and talk with the competitors. Either way, you'll get motivated and inspired.

Trade shows are also huge networking opportunities and they provide ample exposure to a wealth of specialty products, equipment, and tools. They're like a giant playground for food industry professionals, only they're as much about being serious as they are about having fun.

#96: Keep Volunteering

As long as you're in a kitchen, whether at the bottom or the top, you should never stop volunteering. When you're just starting out, volunteering for industry events like the StarChefs.com International Chefs Congress or charity events like Taste of The Nation will give you experience and exposure. When you've gained experience, volunteering allows you to share your wisdom with up-and-comers and to give back by using your name and talent to generate funds for worthy causes.

Top Chef Master, Chef-Owner of Red Rooster, and C-CAP Board Member Marcus Samuelsson once told me, "I can never forget where I came from, nor can I ever forget how many people in this world have so little while relatively few have so much. For these reasons, I'll always work for charitable causes."

#97: Continuing Ed & Certifications

Whether or not you went to culinary school, once you're out in the workforce, there's no reason to stop studying. That's what formal continuing education classes are all about; the never-ending pursuit of knowledge and skills.

You can easily seek out intensive, short-term classes for specialized skills like cake decorating, working with chocolate and sugar, making bread, sushi, or fresh pasta, honing your knife skills, and even learning about wine.

There are also a number of professional certifications you can attain as you gain more and more knowledge and experience. The American Culinary Federation offers all levels of certifications for chefs and pastry chefs, as does the Culinary Institute of America. You can even become certified in kitchen sanitation and safety, which at the beginning of your career can make you an above-average commodity on job hunts because every kitchen needs a sanitation-certified employee on staff during every shift.

#98: Self-Promotion

If you're not willing to promote yourself, then you can't expect others to promote you. This new dimension of culinary careers today may make some budding chefs (and even well-established ones), feel more than a little uncomfortable. Still, the fact is that being a chef today is a hot career with potentially enormous rewards and undeniably cut-throat competition.

Self-promotion doesn't have to mean creating an in-your-face website full of self-satisfying photos or starting a self-serving chef blog, but it can mean having a creative website showcasing your work or an interesting, informative chef blog sharing what matters most to you.

Shuna Lydon, Executive Pastry Chef at Peels NYC and an award-winning blogger who never went to culinary school, started eggbeater just because she had a desire to blog, not because she was thinking of self-promotion. When I asked her about the relationship between eggbeater and her career success, she told me, "Eggbeater has helped me in my career, yes, but in more subtle ways than seem obvious. Future employers do not "find me" via eggbeater. I find my own jobs. But name recognition comes when someone looks for you on the internet and they find so many links that they realize you must know what you're doing!"

It must be said that the degree to which you self-promote or create a public image is going to and should depend on your own personal definition of success as well as how much you want to put your name and face out there. Every year in Paris a prestigious competition is held for the best croissant in the city. One year, when the winner was revealed, the judges opened the entry paper and instead of finding a name, they found an anonymous entry with these words: "To this baker, the happiness of his customers is all the recognition he needs."

#99: Keep Learning

Beyond formal continuing education classes, there's the ever-expanding opportunity to simply learn from your peers and colleagues. Never assume you know everything there is to know because you definitely won't improve your skills with that attitude. Get to know the work of other chefs, travel, spend time in their shops and kitchens, and learn from everyone you meet.

Ewald Notter, world-renowned sugar and chocolate artist, author, Coupe du Monde de la Pâtisserie champion, and director of The Notter School of Pastry Arts in Orlando, Florida, once said to me, "Even today I must keep learning. I still travel to other schools and go into other pastry kitchens around the world because there's always some new technique, new tool, new product that I haven't seen and that will continue to make me a better pastry chef and teacher. If I don't keep learning, then I can't keep creating."

APPENDIX A:

WORKSHEETS

Notes to Self:

Notes to Self:

Notes to Self:

Notes to Self:

Notes to Self:

Notes to Self:

APPENDIX B:

RESOURCES

National Restaurant Association
http://www.restaurant.org/

James Beard Foundation
http://www.jamesbeard.org/

Careers through Culinary Arts Program (C-CAP)
http://www.ccapinc.org/

U.S. Department of Education Student Loans
http://www.direct.ed.gov/

The American Culinary Federation
http://www.acfchefs.org

www.StarChefs.com

ABOUT

THOMAS SCHAUER

THE AUTHOR

REGINA VAROLLI grew up in the restaurant business. The daughter of a restaurateur mom and a chef dad, she feels most at home in kitchens and restaurants. Regina is a regular contributor to Huffington Post Food and a freelance food, wine, and travel writer. She is also the Founder and CEO of CulinaryEpicenter, a website and company devoted to strengthening the careers of anyone working their way to the top of the culinary and hospitality industry.

Available Titles in the 99 Series®

www.99-Series.com

CPSIA information can be obtained at www.ICGtesting.com
Printed in the USA
LVOW12s1245121214

418551LV00001B/38/P